F IN

EXAMS

THE BEST ENGLISH, GEOGRAPHY,
HISTORY AND SCIENCE BLUNDERS

Richard Benson

summersdale

F IN EXAMS

Summersdale Publishers Ltd
46 West Street
Chichester
West Sussex
PO19 1RP
UK

www.summersdale.com

Printed and bound in India by Nutech Print Services

ISBN: 978-1-84953-710-0

Substantial discounts on bulk quantities of Summersdale books are available to corporations, professional associations and other organisations. For details telephone Summersdale Publishers on (+44-1243-771107), fax (+44-1243-786300) or email (nicky@summersdale.com).

Contents

F IN English

THE BEST TEST PAPER BLUNDERS

Richard Benson

Introduction

Did your English exams shake you up more than Shakespeare? Thousands of people have relived their exam-day nightmares with *F in Exams* and we just couldn't resist bringing you some more hilarious test paper blunders in this extra-special English edition.

This book is full to the brim with funny answers from clueless but canny students of English which will have you cackling at Coleridge, giggling at grammar, and sniggering at split infinitives. Just don't blame us if your English teacher suspects you can't speak the language...

Subject: **The Classics**

Give an example of sibilance in *Romeo and Juliet*.

Juliet and Tybalt are cousins but I don't think there are any sibilance.

Give a brief summary of the plot of *The Strange Case of Dr Jekyll and Mr Hyde*.

Jekyll and Hyde find a briefcase, and it's very strange.

List the main events of *Robinson Crusoe*.

Robinson goes on a cruise.

In what way is Pip an uncertain hero?

Because he's just not sure.

Provide an example of dramatic irony in *Othello*.

The Classics

What theme does the quote 'as prime as goats, as hot as monkeys' explore?

Dishes from kebab menus.

What is the overall message of *Frankenstein*?

Don't reanimate corpses.

What does *Heart of Darkness* say about the nature of humanity?

It's quite dark in nature
for humans without any
electricity.

What do you think makes Mercutio such a memorable character in *Romeo and Juliet*?

He lives inside a
thermometer

The Classics

Which character famously tilted at windmills?

Donkey Oatie

Paraphrase the events of *Gulliver's Travels*.

Gulliver goes on holiday. He comes back, having enjoyed himself.

 IN ENGLISH

What is the significance of Dr Jekyll's door in *Dr Jekyll and Mr Hyde?*

It's the way he gets into Dr Jekyll's lab.

Why is isolation an important theme in Mary Shelley's *Frankenstein?*

When you're that ugly, isolation becomes a necessity.

Give an example of euphemism in *Midsummer Night's Dream*.

BOTTOM.

What fatal flaws did Theseus struggle with?

The flaw of the labyrinth was really slippery and dangerous.

Provide your best translation into modern English for Chaucer's lines, 'I seye for me, it is a great disese/ Wher-as men han ben in greet welthe and ese/To heren of hir sodeyn fal, allas!'

Ain't it rubbish when mandem
who has got loadsa dough don't
got loadsa dough anymore,
you get me?

Name a key theme in *Madame Bovary*.

Cows

Summarise the events of *The Fall of the House of Usher*.

Building mishaps occur.

Summarise the events of *Paradise Lost*.

God and Satan are arguing over who gets to keep Paradise, but couldn't find it anyway.

What are the main themes from *Sense and Sensibility?*

SENSES AND THE ABILITY TO SENSE THINGS.

The Classics

Explore a key theme from *Wuthering Heights*.

Cliffs

List two major themes of *The Strange Case of Dr Jekyll and Mr Hyde*.

Dr Jekyll. Mr Hyde.

Subject: *English Literature*

How is Piggy made sympathetic in *The Lord of the Flies*?

His little curly tail.

To what was Hemingway referring with the quote 'This isn't fun anymore'?

This exam

From the set texts, give two examples of Attic literature.

'How to Convert a Loft'
and 'Insulation and You'.

What is the significance of the title of Orwell's *Nineteen Eighty-Four*?

That's when it was written.

List one or more characteristics of Gothic literature.

Black nail varnish.

What aspects of a text would structuralist critics look at?

The buildings.

Name one key plot device you might find in a comedy of manners.

A person who does not say 'please' and 'thank you'.

Introduce and explain one perspective of literary criticism.

Self-help books that tell you what's wrong with you and how you can improve it.

List two ways *Pride and Prejudice* can be read.

1. Sitting down, book on lap.

2. Lying down.

What conventions might show a text to be a historical novel?

Historical novels are famous novels

What does it mean when we say a novel is written in the third-person perspective?

There are only three characters.

English Literature

Give an example of a proverb.

A journey of a thousand miles is
as good as a rest to a blind horse
that gathers no moss for want
of a shoe.

Define an epistolary novel.

A novel about religious people.

lalalalala

What factors lead towards Nancy's death in *Oliver Twist*?

Charles Dickens killed her.

Discuss the reasons for the main action of *Of Mice and Men* taking place over four days.

It is a short book, so doesn't take more than four days to read.

Give one famous quote from the play *Hamlet* which makes reference to Yorick?

The grand old duke of Yorick, he had ten thousand men...

Summarise the events of Henry Fielding's *Tom Jones*.

A man becomes a famous singer.

How might the themes of *Crime and Punishment* be relevant to today's society?

It's been adapted into a TV show called Law and Order.

Name two literary genres.

Fiction and non-fiction.

Subject: *English Language*

Name the three tenses.

Stressed, worried and concerned.

Give an example of a sentence containing a suffix.

Suffix to say, I won't be going back there again.

What is a subordinate clause?

It's a very meek clause.

Write a sentence with an example of irony.

When I put my clothes in the wash, my mum brings them back to me all irony.

 IN ENGLISH

Give a brief definition of a split infinitive.

When two people break up and
<u>never</u> get back together.

Write a sentence containing a double negative.

Mike is ugly and he smells.

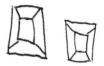

What is a relative clause?

Mrs Santa.

If someone refers to an idiolect, what do they mean?

The opposite of intellect.

When would you use a preposition?

When you want to
marry someone.

Give an example of a connective.

Glue, Blu-tack or Sellotape.

Give an example of an intensifier.

My sister intensifies my feelings of annoyance.

Give an example of form.

The one you fill in to get your
National Insurance card.

On average, how many words a minute do we usually speak?

It varies depending on how annoying you are.

When you articulate you:

Move your hands a lot while you're speaking.

How significant is tone of voice when communicating?

My mum says 'it's not what you said it's the way that you said it.'

Give an example of a request and a gesture you might use to emphasise it.

Get lost please.

What effect does eye contact have when you are talking to someone?

It makes them think you fancy them.

Define 'multimodal' talk.

Talking to two or more models at once

What are we referring to when we refer to the 'Queen's English'?

We're referring to the fact that the Queen _is_ English (and a bit German).

Write a sentence containing a 'question tag'.

I should know what it is, shouldn't I?

Define sociolect.

A violent and dangerous individual with no empathy.

Give an example of a regional accent.

Oo arr missis

Give an example of an exchange between two people containing 'fillers'.

Two old people – their dentures will have fillers.

Define dialect.

Dr Who's biggest enemies were the dialects.

English Language

When people from a particular class share a way of speaking it is called:

Being northern/being southern.

When people from a particular area share a way of speaking it is called:

Inside jokes.

What do we mean by 'mode'?

Grass that's been cut.

Give an example of a sentence with slang in it.

This is an example of a sentence with slang innit.

Give an example of a language routine.

Get up, speak, eat dinner, speak, go to bed.

What are anecdotes an example of?

medicine that you give someone to stop them dying of poison

What are we discussing when we talk about the 'flow'

The direction it
is moving in.

What is a sonnet?

WHAT A MOMMET AND A
POPPET GIVE BIRTH TO.

Subject: *Creative Writing*

When writing to argue, what techniques might you use to gain the readers' attention?

Writing in CAPITAL LETTERS

You should always end a piece of argumentative writing by:

Telling the reader you will slap them if they refuse to agree.

What techniques might you use to gain the reader's sympathy?

Rub onion on the paper to make them cry.

What sort of newspaper article explores opinion rather than facts?

Most.

Give two stylistic features of a column.

GRECIAN. ROMAN.

What does a 'call to action' mean?

When you get made to go to war.

Creative Writing

What is a recreation?

Sport is an example of recreation, such as tennis or yoga.

Give two techniques writers use to create atmosphere.

A few drinks.
Some good friends.

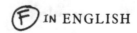

What is a 'dangling participle'?

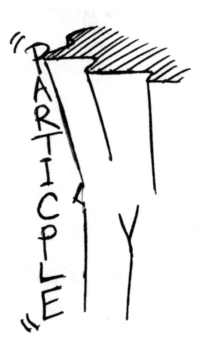

Why should an author keep their audience in mind?

Because if they kept them in real life that would be kidnapping.

Give the correct opening for writing a formal letter to a person you don't know.

Opening: 'Who are you?'

What effect can a rhetorical question have?

Irritation

What is a strap line?

When you get sunburnt wearing
a strappy top and have white
lines on your shoulders.

Creative Writing

What is a headline?

The line on your head
where your hat was
too tight.

What sort of terms are 'you have to', 'you must' and 'you ought to'?

The sort my mum uses too often

What is the purpose of writing to advise?

you can tell people what to do and they can't say no.

What is the effect of imperatives?

They make you poo

Creative Writing

Give an example of an 'impersonal' instruction.

I don't know you, but lend me a tenner.

When might you use a conditional phrase?

When washing your hair, after the shampoo phrase.

Give an example of a group of three.

Athos, Porthos and Aramis.

Give two examples of presentational devices.

Smart board. Pointer

Creative Writing

GAP stands for:

fashionable clothes at affordable prices.

Define 'embody'.

The thing beneath
Em's head.

← Emhead
← Embody

 IN ENGLISH

Define 'discourse marker'.

If you get any on your clothes while you're writing with it, it will wash off.

What does PEE stand for?

It's like pee, but when you're really desperate.

Give an example of a 'purpose'.

They're quite like
dolphins.

Define 'ambiguity'.

The point of ambiguity is that it
can't be defined.

Write a sentence that tells the reader about a character using the rule 'show don't tell'.

Subject: **Poetry and Drama**

Using the works you have studied, give an example of a heroic couplet.

BATMAN & ROBIN.

What is a roundel?

Similar to a squarel...
but circle shaped.

Poetry and Drama

How is 'Sonnet 34' a formal poem?

Because it is numbered.

What effect can alliteration have?

Makes the streets look untidy.

 IN ENGLISH

Give an example of a poetic form.

A poet's driving licence application.

What is a villanelle?

A place where villains
go when they die.

What is a simile?

What is poetic meter?

One hundred centimetres of poem.

Give ONE example of a famous ode.

Ode cologne.

Give a brief definition of blank verse.

PAGE CONTAINING
BLANK VERSE.

PAGE

Using the set texts, discuss ONE theme shared by the poems.

They're all set texts.

Define 'physical theatre'.

A building, normally quite big, with a stage and seats and an expensive bar.

Poetry and Drama

What is 'Commedia dell'arte'?

It's a high-class sitcom.

When might an author use 'anti-climax'?

It's to be used with anti-freeze.

What is melodrama?

It's the opposite of
an angry drama.

MELON-DRAMA!

Poetry and Drama

In poetry, what is the 'voice'?

Someone who reads it out loud.

In poetry, what is a fourteener?

A teenage poet.

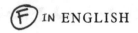

What is a stanza?

Italian book stand

Explore one work by Seigfried Sassoon.

He invented a bob in the 60s.

What is an epitaph?

A swear word.

Define repertoire.

When you keep saying
the same thing over and
over and over.

What does the term 'blocking' mean to a playwright?

When the characters stop each other from doing what they want to.

What themes are important to a Modernist poet?

Technology.

What is a canto?

Faster than a trot.

What made Imagist poets different to other poets writing at the time?

They drew pictures instead of writing words.

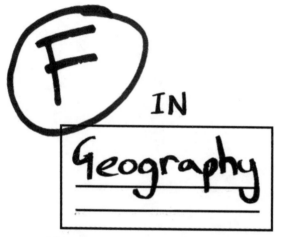

F IN Geography

THE BEST TEST PAPER BLUNDERS

Richard Benson

Introduction

Did your Geography exams involve confusion between your Andes and your Pyrenees? Thousands of people have relived their exam-day nightmares with *F in Exams*, and we just couldn't resist bringing you some more hilarious test paper blunders in this globe-trotting Geography edition.

This book is full to the brim with funny answers from clueless but canny students of geography which will have you cackling at continental drift, chuckling at climate, and howling hysterically at human geography. Just don't blame us if your geography teacher sends you on a one-way trip to the naughty corner…

Subject: **Climates & Environments**

Where can you find the Andes?

Google Earth.

What is the difference between biotic and abiotic factors in an ecosystem?

A.

What methods are used for preserving rainforest?

Pickling

What is afforestation?

When the train stops in the forests.

wwww

Why can flooding be beneficial?

If you're on fire

Describe two negative effects of a drought.

1. No swimming
2. No wet T-shirt competitions.

Where are temperate deciduous forests found?

In places that are not too hot or cold.

What are plants that are able to store water called?

Clever.

Where are deserts found?

In the chilled
aisle

What is salinisation?

Cleaning.

What does the term 'glaciation' refer to?

A FOOD PROCESS —

E.G. GLACIATED CHERRIES.

What is the name for the long lakes found at the bottom of deep glacial valleys?

Geoff & Harry.

Name one cause of avalanches.

Yodelling

How are sedimentary rocks formed?

That's sedimentary my
dear Watson.

Photos of the Alps show that glaciers have retreated over the last 50 years. One reason for this could be climate change. What could another reason be?

They're shy.

Describe the greenhouse effect.

When you get old and spend
all your time in the
greenhouse, tending plants.

Why is it helpful to leave dead wood to rot?

Because if you use it to
build things it breaks.

What were the main exports of Persia?

Cats and rugs

Turkey has seen a fall in its levels of export trade. Give one possible reason for this.

A rise in vegetarianism — turkeys being eaten less.

What does a choropleth map show?

location of choropleths.

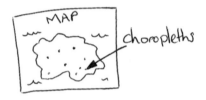

MAP

choropleths

Where would you find the Pyrenees?

In the mountains.

Climates & Environments

Everest base camp is an example of an extreme environment visited by tourists. Give two reasons why tourists visit extreme environments.

1. They didn't read the brochure
2. They want to impress their friends

Give two reasons people would visit Iceland.

1. Cheap food
2. Good advertising.

What is meant by a 'fragile environment'?

A glass house

Why do people continue to live in areas affected by tropical storms?

Good schools, off-road parking, quiet neighbours.

Subject: .... **The Coast & Rivers** ....

What does it mean if a waterfall has an overhang?

Not enough exercise, too many chips

What is the hydrological cycle also known as?

Clever water bike.

How much of the world's water is stored in seas and oceans?

A LOT.

What is the drainage basin?

A sink without a plug.

What is a confluence?

When two things
happen at the same
time, unexpectedly.

What is the mouth of a river?

It is how the river
eats.

What is an oxbow lake?

A lake protected by a cow that's good at archery.

What is the watershed?

Where fish do DIY.

Describe the process of abrasion.

It's a way to cook steak.

What is created when a river runs over alternating layers of hard and soft rock?

Glam rock.

Name one key force of change in a coastal system.

THE R.N.L.I.

How are waves created?

1. Lift your arm.
2. Shake your hand back and forth.

What is the distance a wave has travelled called?

The sea.

When does a constructive wave occur?

When I do well on sports day and mum waves and shouts 'well done'.

When is deposition likely to occur?

When you are at the bank

What are wooden barriers built at right-angles to the beach called?

fences.

What is it called when areas of coastline are allowed to erode and then flood naturally?

Laziness

What is a storm surge?

When the gods get angry.

 IN GEOGRAPHY

Name a way of protecting a coastal area from flooding.

Armed police

What is the direction of longshore drift?

UP.

The Coast & Rivers

There are many different ways in which the sea erodes the coast. Explain two ways in which the sea erodes the coast.

1. Nibbling
2. Biting

Describe one key difference between destructive and constructive waves.

Constructive waves are constructive. Destructive waves are destructive.

Explain the causes of cliff recession along the UK coastline.

Nobody will pay to see him any more, not even in Blackpool.

Some people agree with the building of coastal defences while others disagree with it. Why is this?

Some people will disagree with anything.

What is the purpose of dams?

Similar to blast
and gah.

What is a groyne?

A noise of pain.

Subject:  How the Earth Works

What environmental factors can cause plate slippage?

Loose table legs.

What is slumping?

Bad posture.

How old is the Earth?

Years.

What do the geological time periods relate to?

We have geography at 11am on Wednesdays and Fridays.

Which part of the Earth is directly below the crust?

The filling

Describe the different phases of the rock cycle.

It developed from Rythym and Blues and Jazz, into Rock 'n' Roll and then into Rock.

What is the more common name for kaolin?

Ninja.

Name a characteristic of metamorphic rock.

Changeable.

Name a characteristic of igneous rock.

Very clever.

Which part of the Earth is the hottest?

Africa.

Give two differences between continental crust and oceanic crust.

One is on French pizza, the other is on seafood pizza.

How are fold mountains formed?

Origami.

What causes earthquakes?

Volcanoes.

Give two ways in which people can be prepared for earthquakes.

1. HOLD ON TIGHT.
2. GET IN A ZORBING BALL.

What is the name for professionals who monitor and predict volcanic eruptions?

Vulcans

Give an example of a supervolcano.

Describe the likely worldwide effects of a supervolcano eruption.

Death.
Dinosaurs.

What is a tsunami?

a move in
sumo wrestling

What is the name for the scientific practice of studying the atmosphere and monitoring and predicting the weather and climate?

Being a weather man.

Where do hurricanes normally form?

In the air.

Which part of the British Isles experiences the shortest days during the winter and the longest days during the summer?

France

What is meant by extreme weather?

When you have to stay indoors

How the Earth Works

December 2010 is one example of extreme weather in the UK. What was December 2010 a period of?

Winter

Draw an annotated diagram to explain the process of relief rainfall.

How does temperature differ at a high altitude, compared to temperature at a low altitude?

It's higher at high altitudes and lower at low altitudes.

What does the term latitude refer to?

It's French for attitude

Subject: Human Geography One — Urban Life & Systems

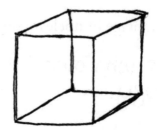

What public services does a youthful population put a strain on?

Beer
Traffic cones
Shopping trollies

What is a disadvantage of nuclear power?

The people who own it might get power crazy.

Explain the increase in demand for water and electricity in the south of England.

They're thirsty and keep getting bigger TVs.

Why does population naturally change over time?

It gets bored.

Describe two ways of reducing the demand for water.

1. When it's yellow let it mellow
2. When it's brown flush it down.

What is meant by the term 'carbon footprint'?

Someone who steps in soot has them.

What tends to happen to a country's carbon footprint
as it develops?

IT GETS DARKER.

What does feedback in an industrial system involve?

A loud, high-pitched noise.

What is secondary industry?

Not as good as primary industry.

Which sector employs the most people in the UK?

The job sector.

Name a factor which might attract a multinational corporation to a country.

Nice beaches.

What is it called when a foreign country invests in a country?

Investment

Name a negative impact of globalisation.

You can never see the bits at the top
and bottom where the frame goes:

Name two economic indicators.

Left blinker and right blinker.

What does the term population distribution refer to?

The spread of fizzy drinks throughout the country.

What is meant by population density?

How stupid people are.

How many people could there be on the planet by 2025?

None — the world will end in 2017

Describe one major problem caused by counter-urbanisation.

The urbanisers might get angry.

What is a 'migrant'?

A really bad headache.

Migration from a country may have both positive and negative effects. Describe these effects.

Positive - Moving somewhere nice
Negative - Moving somewhere horrible

Describe some ways that pollution problems could be reduced in cities in poorer parts of the world.

Get rid of the cows.

What does CBD stand for?

Currently Bored Dizzy

Explain why the number of food miles is increasing.

PEOPLE DEMAND FREE -RANGE, SO
THE CHICKENS RUN MORE MILES
EVERY DAY.

What is GNP?

A far right
Political party

Many countries now have an ageing population. Give two problems which may be caused by an ageing population.

Shortage of light blue hair dye.
Longer queues on pension day.

Subject: Human Geography Two
Rural Life & Sustainability

What is a nucleated village?

One that's close to a nuclear power station.

What factors affect the sustainability of food sources?

How much people like the taste of them.

Describe reasons for the change in the rural-urban fringe.

Drunken haircuts.

Describe the process of irrigation.

When a farmer irritates his crops they grow faster

Which type of feature is Watlowes an example of?

A cut-price supermarket.

Give a reason for the decline in employment in primary and secondary industries in the UK.

Less children.

Name one advantage of quarrying.

Any disagreements are out in the open
and can be dealt with.

Name one disadvantage of quarrying.

Sometimes it ends in tears, or blows.

Name one way in which the impact of quarrying can be reduced.

Softer hammers.

What can a quarry be used for after the rock has been extracted?

Film sets.

What is a brownfield site?

A site with no grass,
just mud.

Explain the terms 'subsistence farming' and 'nomadic farming'.

One is underground and
the other is done by gnomes.

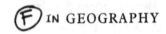

Give one positive aspect of organic farming.

The organic labels look prettier

What is meant by 'pull' and 'push' factors?

How strong the teams are in a tug of war.

What is meant by 'factory farming'?

Growing factories.

What is 'agri-business'?

A bad way of running your business as you might lose customers.

What is the difference between 'hard' and 'soft' engineering techniques?

The consistency.

The tourist industry has grown rapidly during the last 50 years. Give reasons for this rapid growth.

More tourists

Describe the characteristics of shanty houses.

1. Near the seaside
2. Full of people who like singing

The development of greenfield sites can threaten the countryside. Explain why this can be the case.

Greenfield sites are very aggressive.

What is urbanisation?

More people listening to R'n'B.

Explain two possible causes of rural depopulation.

1. No-one fancies farmers
2. People leave because the countryside smells funny.

What is meant by 'the development gap'?

The time it takes for you to get your photos back from the shop.

Explain the difference between standard of living and quality of life.

It's the difference between home brand cola and the real thing.

What is 'stewardship'?

Difficult times for beef stews, lamb stews etc.

What is meant by the term ecotourism?

Travelling to Bognor Regis by coach.

F IN History

THE BEST TEST PAPER BLUNDERS

Richard Benson

Introduction

Do you remember the Dark Ages? No, not your school days but the subject of many dreary History lessons? Thousands of people have relived their exam-day nightmares with *F in Exams*, and we just couldn't resist bringing you some more hilarious test paper blunders in this epoch-making History edition.

This book is full to the brim with funny answers from clueless but canny students of history which will have you cackling over Kings, hooting at invading hordes and wheezing at the World Wars! Just don't blame us if your History teacher puts you in the stocks…

Subject: **Major Conflicts**

What was the Kellogg-Briand pact?

Mr Briand had to agree not to make cereal anymore because Mr Kellogg didn't like the competition.

Name three members of the League of Nations.

Arsenal, AC Milan and Bayern.

How might the outcome of Hitler and Chamberlain's meeting at Bad Godesberg have been improved?

It could've been held at Good Godesberg.

What was the issue with the League of Nations' Secretariat?

SHE WAS RUBBISH AT FILING.

Why did the British public want more Dreadnoughts?

To balance out the
Dreadcrosses

Major Conflicts

What is the significance of the 1889 German Navy Cabinet?

It had brass handles and a false bottom.

What was the armistice?

It's similar to legistice, but for arms.

Name two causes of the Cold War.

1. Soldiers with runny noses.
2. Soldiers with coughs.

What was the U2 incident?

The Edge stole Bono's sunglasses.

Major Conflicts

What was the cause of the Hungarian Revolution in 1956?

THEY WERE GETTING HUNGARIER AND HUNGARIER

What was the Truman Doctrine?

A more trustworthy version of the Falseman Doctrine.

What do the letters NATO stand for?

Not At The Office

What problem rocked the USSR in 1986?

The Beatles

Major Conflicts

What is hyperinflation?

*When a bouncy castle is blown up so much
if you jumped on it it would burst*

Give an example of semi-successful propaganda.

The only way is Essex.

Who were the members of the Big Three?

King Kong, Godzilla and
The Hulk.

What is Appel Quay famous for?

Opening Appel Door.

Major Conflicts

Give a brief summary of events of the Beagle Conflict.

Many Beagles lost their lives.

What was the cause of the Gallic Wars?

A gallic bread shortage.

Provide a summary of the events of the Boston Tea Party.

Everyone had a cup of tea and some cake.

Major Conflicts

What makes the 5 November a significant date in history?

The rhyme tells us to remember it.

What was the cause of the Boxer Rebellion?

The Boxers weren't being paid enough.

What were the terms of the Treaty of Versailles?

AUTUMN TERM, SPRING TERM, SUMMER TERM

What happens when a country demilitarises?

Its citizens lose motivation and feel low.

Why was the 'Glorious' Revolution of 1688 called such?

Because it was just fabulous, darling.

What was the Crimean War?

A war against criminals.

Subject: **Kings and Queens**

What is an interregnum?

A small snack between meals.

In regards to Henry VIII, what is the rhyme 'divorced, beheaded, died, divorced, beheaded, survived' about?

Death, divorce and survival.

How did William the Conqueror get his moniker?

He went to the opticians.

Kings and Queens

Name two advantages Oliver Cromwell's New Model Army had over Charles I's Royalists.

They were plastic so they never got hurt.

What was the purpose of the Domesday Book?

People in olden times were quite superstitious and they would predict the end of the world.

Provide two names that Elizabeth I was known by.

'Your Majesty' and
'Please Don't Cut My Head Off.'

What was the role of the Lord Protector?

Protecting the Lord

Kings and Queens

What was the War of the Roses regarding?

Trying to stop the greenfly eating them.

For what reason was James I also known as James VI?

They couldn't count.

 IN HISTORY

Name two attributed qualities of Richard the Lionheart.

He had long flowing hair and sharp teeth.

What was Harold II defending in the Battle of Hastings?

Hastings.

How did King Cnut reprove his courtiers?

He cnutted them.

Who were the Princes in the Tower?

Rapunzel and Sleeping Beauty are two
Princes that lived in a tower.

Name one great achievement of Charlemagne.

Inventing sparkling wine.

For what reason did Boadicea revolt against the Romans?

THEY KEPT PRONOUNCING HER NAME WRONG

Kings and Queens

What was Hugh Despenser's place in the court of Edward II?

Giving out snacks and cold drinks.

What was the House of Tudor?

It had a white front with black beams and low doors.

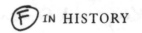

How did Mary I get the nickname 'Bloody Mary'?

From the drink.

Against who did Robert the Bruce defend Scotland?

Macbeth.

Kings and Queens

Why was James II known as the Great Pretender?

He was the most talented member of the Pretenders.

Who was Anne of Cleves?

A German lady with a big knife.

Why was George IV called the 'first gentleman of England'?

He always put the toilet seat down.

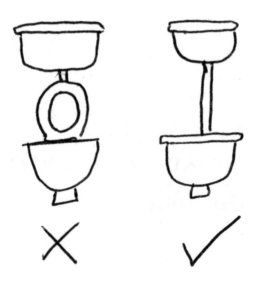

What was the Crystal Palace?

Football Team

Why was the Assembly of the Notables formed?

It was a minute-taking society.

Subject: ....**Twentieth Century History**.......

Name the five Giants of Poverty.

Jolly Green Giant, BFG, Hagrid, Beanstalk Giant & Gulliver.

What was the agreement made through the Lib-Lab pact of 1903?

People could wear flip-flops to work.

What was the subject of the Beveridge report?

Hot drinks

What, or who, were the Suffragettes?

60's pop group.

Where were the effects of the Depression least felt?

At the top of mountains.

Give a brief description of the 'never-never'.

Where Peter Pan lives.

What is public health?

> Anything involving eating
> apples outdoors or running
> in parks.

What is a census?

> Latin for a hundred.

What happened to heavy industries during the Depression?

They got heavier, as people eat when depressed.

What was the Special Areas Act?

Something very rude.

What was the purpose of the labour exchange?

So people could try each other's jobs for a while.

Give a consequence of the General Strike.

There were no Generals to run the army.

Give a brief description of the events of 'Red Friday'.

It followed 'Really Sunny But No Sun Cream Thursday'.

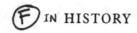

What is Social Engineering?

Inventions like Facebook and Twitter.

What caused the fall of the Berlin Wall in 1989?

Shoddy Pointing.

What was said to be the last defence against extreme poverty?

Winning the lottery.

What were the consequences of the 1765 Stamp Act?

Fair postage for all.

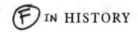

What was the Belle Epoque period?

Before Bella met Edward or Jacob there was a time she dated Epoque

How did the flying shuttle revolutionise the textile industry?

They could use new materials from space.

What was the Wall Street Crash?

A CAR MOUNTED THE PAVEMENT $ HIT THE WALL

What is another name for the 'Roaring Twenties'?

The shouting Post-Teens.

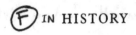

Give a definition of a co-operative society.

A VILLAGE OF PEOPLE THAT
LIKE TO SHOP AT THEIR LOCAL
STORE.

Define the proto-industrialisation movement.

A project to create factories built
by microbes.

What sort of engine was the table engine?

It keeps your food warm.

What is the poverty line?

It goes round the middle of the earth.

What were the events leading up to the St Valentine's Day Massacre?

Someone didn't get any cards.

Subject: General History

Name the four humours of Greek medicine.

Slapstick, irony, wordplay and poo jokes.

In Ancient Greece, where did the clinical observation of a patient with an illness begin?

At the doctor's

What was Vegetius famous for?

His healthy diet.

In Medieval England, what was a reredorter?

Someone who comes in to
decorate after the first time goes
wrong.

What is meant by the term 'prehistoric'?

Before anyone cared
enough to write it down.

What is the Hippocratic Oath?

An oath you don't intend to keep.

What is the 'Ides of March' famous for?

Unusual patterns in the March seas.

What is the definition of a 'quack' doctor?

One that specialises in ducks.

Who was the Ancient Egyptian God of Death?

A newbie.

Who were the visigoths?

Fans of The Cure in hi-vis vests.

Imsety, Hapy and Duamutef are examples of what?

The seven dwarfs.

List three notable features of Gaulish society.

Asterix, Obelix and
Cacofonix.

What language did the Romans write in?

Roman.

What was the significance of Hadrian's Wall?

It was the first ever wall.

What did an Ancient Egyptian embalmer do?

Embalmed Ancient Egyptians.

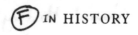

Name one characteristic of the Enlightenment.

Brightness.

Describe an Ionic column.

A column that's deliberately contrary to its expected meaning.

Describe an amphitheatre.

A place where frogs hold plays

What technological advances did Rome bring to Britain?

Roman candles.

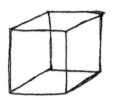

What are Picts an example of?

A tool for mining.

What is the Upper Palaeolithic?

A dinosaur's thigh bone.

Give an example of Megafauna.

A giant baby deer.

Why is the Early Stone Age contemporaneous with the Lower Palaeolithic?

They just don't get on well together.

What were flintknappers?

They stole flint and demanded a ransom for its safe return.

Define carbon dating.

It's how scientists work out the age of carbon.

What contributed to the Bronze Age collapse?

Rust.

Subject: **Politics**..

Politics

What were the events of the Fashoda Crisis?

Lots of people turned up to a party in the same dress.

What was the Easter Rising?

The tradition of cooking Hot Cross Buns for Easter.

Why was Spinning Jenny phased out?

She got dizzy.

What were the Swing Rioters of 1830 protesting against?

Jazz.

Politics

Give a brief description of the Rump Parliament.

It was held inside the Trousers of Commons.

What was the purpose of the Barebones Parliament?

They provide a skeleton staff when other politicians are on holiday.

What was the position of the Whigs in the 18th Century?

On top of bald people's heads.

Politics

What factors contributed to the fall of the British Empire?

Everybody got bored of eating fish and chips all the time.

What was the Lytton Commission reporting on?

Picking up rubbish

 IN HISTORY

What was Britain's interest in the Suez Canal?

That's where Suez pudding comes from.

What was known as the Pax Britannica?

British sanitary products.

Give a brief description of the Malthusian Trap theory.

You put cheese in the trap.

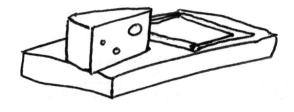

For what is the Order of the Garter awarded?

Holding up stockings.

Why were the Corn Laws repealed?

When they were pealed the first time there were bits left on them.

What was Chamberlain's plan for appeasement?

That peas should be
served alongside fish
and chips.

What event occurred under the Elementary Education
Act of 1870?

Sherlock Holmes became
required reading in Schools

Name two Dissenting groups.

SUGAR AND GRAVY CUBES
BOTH DISSENT IN WATER

What were the reasons for the March of the Blanketeers?

They were poor and couldn't afford duvets.

How is a polytheistic society different to a monotheistic society?

They use better filling in their walls.

Why was the Pains and Penalties Bill introduced in 1820?

To standardise footballing laws.

What was the Poor Law Act of 1388?

It made it illegal to be poor.

What is the definition of an Oligarchy?

A Society where ugly people are in charge.

Politics

To what extent to you agree that the Speenhamland System helped mitigate rural poverty?

They sold more pigs.

Name one of the main principles behind Chartism.

It's an unreasonable fear of charts.

F IN

Science

THE BEST TEST PAPER BLUNDERS

Richard Benson

Introduction

Does thinking about Science exams bring up confusing memories of currents and currants, igneous rock and iguanas? Thousands of people have relived their exam-day nightmares with *F in Exams*, and we just couldn't resist bringing you some more hilarious test paper blunders in this lab-coated Science edition.

This book is full to the brim with funny answers from clueless but canny students of science which will have you chuckling over chemistry, howling at human biology and in peals of laughter over physics! Just don't blame us if your science teacher tells you to come back when you're more evolved…

Subject: **The Natural World**

Different living organisms reproduce in different ways. Describe two methods of reproduction.

The Stork and Angel Gabriel

What is meant by microorganism?

A very small keyboard

The Natural World

How does the process of natural selection work?

The two captains just have to go with their instincts to pick their teams.

What is a genetically modified organism?

Something like a wig which has been made to make a bald person look like they have hair.

What are the properties of crude oil?

It's rude and has no manners.

What are the negative effects of global dimming?

Everybody gets thicker

What are the effects of rearing cattle?

Getting kicked in the teeth.

A phototropism involves a reaction to…

Having your picture taken (near the Equator)

Explain the process of evolution.

How do lichens indicate levels of air pollution?

semaphore

What is likely to happen to an individual that is poorly suited to its environment?

Be bought a new suit

Why are white peppered moths likely to be more common than black ones in country areas?

Racism.

Why was Lamarck's theory of evolution discredited?

Because no one knew who he was.

What causes tectonic plates to move?

Noisy neighbours.

Which is the most abundant gas in the atmosphere?

farts.

Why are coal, oil and natural gas non-renewable resources?

Because they always move on once their contract is up.

What is meant by the term 'biodiversity'?

IT'S A DOUBLE UNIVERSITY

The Natural World

Describe the properties of a meteor.

An animal that only eats meat.

The island of Madagascar houses many species that are not found anywhere else on the planet. Give one possible explanation for this.

Why would they Move? Madagascar is ace!

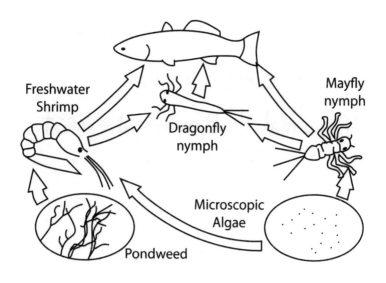

Freshwater
Shrimp

Dragonfly
nymph

Mayfly
nymph

Microscopic
Algae

Pondweed

In this food web, what is represented by the arrows?

Who fancies who.

There has been a marked rise in the percentage of carbon dioxide in the Earth's atmosphere over the last 50 years; suggest one reason for this.

Breathing.

Frog numbers are falling rapidly. Explain the effect this will have on the insect population.

They will have a party.

What is chlorophyll?

An ingredient in
expensive shampoo.

Explain the process of eutrophication.

It's when a country joins
the Euro.

The Natural World

Describe the purpose of cytoplasm.

In Ghostbusters II it was used to make the Statue of Liberty come to life. I've never seen it used since.

What is the purpose of amylase?

It lets people called Amy relax.

Subject: ....Chemistry....

Chemistry

What is the unit 'Calorie' used to measure?

How much somebody will complain about their weight.

Describe a neutrino.

The opposite of an oldtrino.

Define an alloy.

The fancy bit on a car wheel.

What is a polymer?

A group of mermaids.

What is the purpose of chromatography?

To take pictures of time.

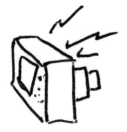

Describe two types of 'smart' material.

Fish and fruit help
Make you smart.

What nutrient is known for helping to produce healthy bones and teeth?

Bread crusts
(that's what my granny says)

Chemistry

What would be the best way to neutralise the effects of acid rain?

Alkaseltzer.

An element has the electronic structure 2,8,4. Which group is it in?

Steps.

Explain the term 'half-life'.

When someone only goes out and has fun half the time.

Describe a radioisotope.

A device for listening to the stars

Chemistry

Why is sodium stored under oil?

So it doesn't have as far to fall if you knock the packet over.

What happens to iron oxide in a blast furnace?

It gets hot

 IN SCIENCE

What does an ionic bond involve?

AN ION AND AN
IRONING BOARD

What does a covalent bond involve?

a secret friendship between nuns

What does phytomining involve?

Mines and a boxing ring.

In comparison with large hydrocarbons, how would you describe small hydrocarbons?

They are smaller.

What process is used to purify copper?

Exorcism.

Why are potassium and sodium in the same group in the periodic table?

Because they are BFFs.

Where are vegetable oils found?

In the oils aisle.

What is mayonnaise an example of?

Salad dressing.

 IN SCIENCE

Define a super-saturated solution.

Water with extra
water in it.

Give an example of an emulsion.

Dulux

What is the symbol for iron?

My Mum does this.

What is the purpose of a fractioning column?

A column with fractions is useless, because it wouldn't hold anything up.

What is an artificial pesticide?

Someone who is only pretending to be annoying really.

Subject: **Physics**

Why are catalytic converters fitted to cars?

To make sure no cats get run over.

What is beta radiation?

Radiation that's nearly complete, but needs to be tested.

Physics

What is a step-up transformer?

It's the sequel to Step Up and Transformers where the humans teach the robots to dance.

Explain how a vehicle can be designed to reduce friction.

It could secrete grease.

Draw the electronic component symbol for a switch.

Earth is closer to the Sun than Mars, and bigger. What are two other differences between the two planets?

1. Colour.
2. Aliens.

Explain the difference between a discrete variable and a categoric variable.

Discrete variables are quite secretive where as categoric variables are rather blunt.

When conducting a study, what is the purpose of a control group?

To tell the others what to do.

Explain the process of thermal energy transfer.

Cuddles

Physics

Explain the difference between potential energy and useful energy.

Potential energy talks a lot but doesn't do much. Useful energy is less fun but more helpful.

What is the distance from the crest of one wave to the crest of the next wave called?

The sea.

Describe the properties of a thermosoftening plastic.

It gets soft when you put it in a flask with hot tea.

What is viscosity a measure of?

HOW SEE-THROUGH YOUR STRETCHY CLOTHES ARE.

Physics

At the end of a marathon, a runner covers herself in a silvered space blanket. Explain how the space blanket helps keep the runner warm.

Alien technology.

Give one advantage, in any research project, of having a large sample size rather than a small sample size.

You can see it better.

Van   Car

The diagram shows a van and a car. The two vehicles have the same mass and identical engines. Explain why the top speed of the car is greater than the top speed of the van.

It has go-faster stripes.

Physics

When taking an X-ray, why does the radiographer go behind a screen?

Privacy.

Explain the advantage of a CT scan compared to an X-ray.

It has more letters.

Explain how a transformer works.

It's a truck, then, it's a robot.

Name one key use of a plane mirror.

CHECK YOUR HAIR LOOKS GOOD AT THE END OF THE JOURNEY.

Physics

Explain the process of bioleaching.

It's when you choose natural bleach.

A student hears the sound waves produced by an ambulance siren. When the ambulance is stationary, the student hears a constant frequency. When the ambulance moves away from the student, the sound they hear changes. What is the name of this effect?

The doppleganger effect.

An astronomer uses a telescope to observe the movement of stars and planets. Give one advantage of having a telescope at the top of a high mountain rather than the bottom.

The Mountain doesn't get in the way.

What is the key use for thermochromic plastic, and why?

To make cool stuff that changes colour.

?

Physics

What is the key use for memory metal, and why?

In guitar solos,
to remember things

What is an electric current?

A zingy fruit.

Subject: **Human Biology**

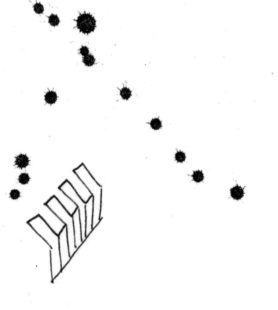

Human Biology

Describe the purpose of antibodies.

They are married to Uncle bodies.

Name four diseases related to diet.

fatness, really fatness, when you're so fat you can't move, death.

What changes take place in a girl during puberty?

SHE GETS BOOBS AND GETS STROPPY.

What is the meaning of the terms 'density dependent' and 'density independent'?

Density dependent is when you are thick and live at home. Density independent is when you are a bit less thick and live on your own.

Human Biology

Where in the human body is the Humerus found?

It changes because everyone's humerus is different.

Give an example of a disease caused by fungi.

Mushroomitis.

What is meant by the term 'placebo effect'?

TECHNICAL TERM FOR WHAT HAPPENS
WHEN PEOPLE GO 'EMO'.

What is the 'metabolic rate'?

Something that makes
cake eaters grow fat.

Describe the function of red blood cells.

To keep blood the right colour.

Describe the function of white blood cells.

Keeps white blood imprisoned.

What is meant by immunity?

You can do bad things and get away with it.

What can vaccination involve?

Going to the beach, Swimming, good food.

It is important to use antibiotics carefully because…

You'll run out of biotics.

What are the key differences between aerobic and anaerobic respiration?

'an'

What is a synapse?

A type of flying dinosaur.

Human Biology

Give two similarities between an eye and a camera.

1. The round bit
2. They both blink.

Give one reason why MRSA is causing problems in hospitals.

Mr. Sa is always causing problems because he is rude and noisy.

What is a fistula?

A mini fist

What is the purpose of plasma?

TVs

Human Biology

Before taking blood, a nurse dabs some alcohol onto the patient's arm. This makes the patient's skin feel cold.

Explain what happens to make the patient's skin feel cold.

A nurse dabs some alcohol
onto the patient's arm.

Coronary heart disease is an illness affected by hereditary factors. Name two hereditary factors that affect our health.

Your mum's health and
your dad's health.

 IN SCIENCE

What causes spots?

Teenagers.

Your body needs to keep an internal temperature of 37°C. Name one way your body cools itself down if your temperature goes above 37°C.

TURNS THE HEATING DOWN

How are inherited factors passed from generation to generation?

By writing a will.

What is the purpose of bile?

When you want to show someone you're angry.

Subject: .... *Science and the Home* ....

Name three domestic sources of carbon dioxide.

1, Mum. 2, Dad. 3, Dog.

What is a pathogen?

Someone who doesn't believe in war.

In 2006, building work began on the UK's largest wind farm at Whitelee in Scotland, consisting of 140 wind turbines with the capacity to generate enough electricity for 200,000 homes.

Give a key reason why this wind farm is unlikely to be able to satisfy the demands of 200,000 homes on a regular basis.

Because homes demand more than wind.

People are likely to object to the building of a wind farm because...

They want all the wind for themselves.

Science and the Home

The Government is investing a lot of money in promoting energy-efficient products. This is because…

…they think this will make people like them.

What purpose is served by the national grid?

It helps when drawing maps.

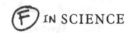

A study found that the use of energy-saving light bulbs actually meant a boiler requires more gas to heat a house.

The most likely explanation for this is that...

They LIED!

By 2020, it is projected that the amount of electricity generated from renewable sources will have doubled from 2005 levels.

The advantage of using more renewable sources of energy is...

People will stop complaining about global warming.

Explain two of the benefits of hydroelectric power stations.

1) It keeps Hydra busy so Hercules can do other things.

2) Hydra's heads grow back, so it's a renewable energy source.

Explain the perceived risks of using Wi-fi.

If you're too enthusiastic at the tennis one you could slap your sister in the face.

Bioethanol is a biofuel. What does this mean?

Here is your answer!

Science and the Home

Despite high fuel costs, it is still cheaper to generate electricity from fossil fuels or nuclear than it is from wind.

This is mainly because…

There are more dead things than wind.

Name a disadvantage of wind farms.

The smell.

Suggest two reasons why it is an advantage to keep farm animals disease free.

Cows are really grumpy
when they're ill and so are
horses.

What is meant by the terms 'hard' and 'soft' water?

Hard water can
beat up soft water

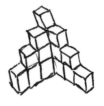

Nuclear power stations generate electricity without burning a fuel.

Name the process by which a nuclear fuel provides the energy needed to generate electricity.

Theft.

What is the advantage of nuclear fuels?

Accidents cause superpowers.

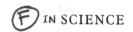

Research was carried out to determine whether there is a link between mobile phone usage and cancer. The £20 million funding for the research came partly from mobile phone companies. Give a reason why some people are concerned that the research was partly paid for by mobile phone companies.

Because they give terrible service.

Explain why the copper pipes inside a solar panel are painted black.

The engineers were big Rolling Stones fans

Science and the Home

Smoking is known to be bad for your health. Give an example of a smoking-related disease.

Coughing.

Suggest why the energy transferred by a television set changes while you are watching it.

You change channel.

Some people worry that living close to electricity pylons might be bad for their health. Why might this be?

Because the people down the road near the pylon are weird.

It is important for our health to have a clean environment in our homes. Name two common pollutants in the home.

1. My brother
2. The dog

Give three common causes of energy loss in the home.

1. Comfy sofas.
2. Soap operas.
3. Mum's big dinners.

Why is it important to carry out a risk assessment before conducting an experiment?

So you know what's going to go wrong.

F IN EXAMS
The Best Test Paper Blunders

Richard Benson

£5.99
Paperback
ISBN: 978-1-84024-700-8

We've all been there. You've been studying hard, the day of the BIG test arrives, you turn over the paper, and 'what the *&%@ does that mean?!' Not a clue. Some students, rather than admit defeat, choose to adopt a more creative approach to answering those particularly awkward exam questions. Packed full of hilarious examples, this book will bring a smile to the face of teachers, parents and students alike – and anyone who's ever had to sit a test.

'*You won't know whether to laugh or cry.*'   Daily Mail

'*Some great examples of exam answers from the most clueless – and inventive – of students.*'   Times Online

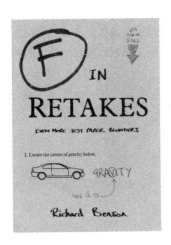

F IN RETAKES
Even More Test Paper Blunders

Richard Benson

£5.99
Paperback
ISBN: 978-1-84953-313-3

The *F in Exams* are over, the results are in and just when you thought it was safe to go back in the classroom… BANG! It's time for *F in Retakes*! Enjoy another heady dose of hilarious answers that canny students have given to the trickiest exam questions.

'Great read. Very funny and definitely worth buying. I would recommend to anyone. Certainly cheered me up! Go get it!'   Amazon reviewer

Featured in *Reveal* magazine and the *Daily Mail*.

F IN SPELLING
The Funniest Test Paper Blunders

Richard Benson

£5.99
Paperback
ISBN: 978-1-84953-649-3

We all know that exams are full of traps for the unwary, especially for those who may not be totally prepared. However, an earnest and creative attempt to answer an awkward question can sometimes lead to hilarious consequences.

This collection of exam howlers and side-splitting spelling slip-ups reveals that there's no reason why ignorance should stop you from coming up with an F-in brilliant answer. Exams will never be the same again!

F IN EXAMS
JOURNAL

Richard Benson

£7.99
Paperback
ISBN: 978-1-84953-650-9

Keep track of all your notes, doodles, scribblings or anything else you could possibly want in this eye-catching journal, peppered with school howlers and ribtickling blunders from the much-loved *F in Exams* series of books.

Have you enjoyed this book?
If so, why not write a review on your favourite website?

If you're interested in finding out more about our books,
find us on Facebook at **Summersdale Publishers**
and follow us on Twitter at **@Summersdale.**

Thanks very much for buying this Summersdale book.

www.summersdale.com